# Canadian
# FESTIVALS

# Canadian
# FESTIVALS

## Susan Hughes

Scholastic Canada Ltd.

Toronto  New York  London  Auckland  Sydney
Mexico City  New Delhi  Hong Kong  Buenos Aires

**Photo credits:**
Cover (Upper, left): Firstlight/Digitalvision; (Upper, right) Firstlight/Corbis; (lower, left) PCL/Alamy; (lower, right) Firstlight/Stockbyte
Back cover (left): Catherine London; (right) © Bruce McGowan /Alamy
Pages iii, 12, 21, 22, 25, 28, 32, 33, 35, 50, 51, 57: istock
Pages 2, 3, 7–11: Catherine London
Page 5: Murray Paulson
Pages 6, 23, 27, 29, 31, 36, 38, 41, 53, 55: Firstlight/Photoresearchers
Page 13, detail: © Brand X Pictures/Alamy
Page 14: © Bruce McGowan/Alamy
Page 16: © Dinodia Images/Alamy
Page 17: © Brand X Pictures/Alamy
Page 19: © John Kershaw/Alamy
Page 40: © VStock/Alamy
Page 43: © Corbis
Page 48: Canstock Photo

Many thanks to Stan Middlestadt at the Ontario Multifaith Council, Janak Burman, Thomas To, Veronica Sullivan and Barbara Hehner for their assistance in reviewing this book.

**Library and Archives Canada Cataloguing in Publication**
Hughes, Susan, 1960-
Canadian festivals / Susan Hughes.
(Canada close up)
ISBN 978-0-439-93923-2
Festivals—Canada—Juvenile literature.
2. Holidays—Canada—Juvenile
literature. I. Title. II. Series: Canada close up
(Markham, Ont.)
GT4813.A2H83 2007      j394.26971      C2006-906677-9

ISBN-10 0-439-93923-2

6  5  4  3  2  1        Printed in Canada        07  08  09  10  11

# Table of Contents

## Pronunciation Guide

We've given you a guide on how to say some of the new words you will find in this book. The syllable that's in **bold** type is stressed, or said a little louder than the others. Here is a key to the vowel sounds in this book:

**ah** as in call; **ay** as in day; **aw** as in lost; **ee** as in see; **eh** as in pet; **eye** as in cry; **o** as in ocean; **oo** as in food; **uh** as in but; **u** as in fur; **i** as in pit; **ow** as in pout.

## Introduction

Celebrate!

In Canada, many people celebrate different holidays and festivals. They remember special people and events that are important to them. They share their faith. They gather with their family and friends. They give thanks.

Here are some of these holidays. They take place at different times throughout the year.

It's festival time!

# Chapter 1

# Eid ul-Fitr

## The End of Ramadan

People of the Islamic faith, called Muslims, look forward to Eid ul-Fitr (**eed** ull-**fit**-ur). It is an important time of rejoicing and celebration.

Eid ul-Fitr is important because it comes at the end of the holy month of Ramadan. Muslims follow a religious calendar that is based on the moon, called a **lunar calendar**. Ramadan is the ninth month of this calendar. It begins when the new crescent moon appears in the sky.

Muslims **fast** during the month of Ramadan. From the time the sun comes up until the time the sun goes down, they do not eat or drink. They think less about their everyday lives and more about their faith.

But each day, after the sun sets, they say a prayer and have a meal, the *iftar*. They visit with friends and family.

**Traditionally, children do not fast during Ramadan.**

☪ The new crescent moon signals the arrival of Eid ul-Fitr.

When Ramadan ends, another crescent moon appears in the sky. This begins the special celebration of Eid ul-Fitr, or the Festival of Fast-Breaking.

Ramadan doesn't begin and end on particular days of the month. It lasts for one cycle of the moon. Ramadan ends when another new crescent moon appears. Usually there is an official announcement made from a local **mosque** (mawsk). Then it is time for the fasting to end — and for Eid to begin!

☾ Families gather for prayers.

During Eid ul-Fitr, Muslims want to thank God for helping them fast for an entire month. They believe their actions and prayers during Ramadan have brought them closer to their faith and the people in their community. They are thankful for the good things in life, like their family and good health.

Every day they say a morning prayer, or *fajr* (fah-**jar**). On the last night of Ramadan, Muslim families may decorate their homes and prepare food for the next day. They get up early on the morning of Eid ul-Fitr.

☾ Muslims greet their family with the words, "***Eid Mubarak***," or "Blessed Eid."

People dress up in their nicest clothes. They may even buy a new set of clothes. They may have a small snack of something sweet, such as dates. Then they go to the mosque or a large centre to attend a special religious service. The congregation gives thanks to God for helping them fast for so many days. It is quite an achievement!

Eid is also a time of forgiveness and a time of giving to others. At Eid, it is important for adults and children to make a generous donation to a charity, such as a gift of food or money. This is called *Zakat-ul-Fitr*. Muslims believe this is a way of serving God.

Sometimes Eid is on a weekday. In Canada, Muslims may plan to take the day off work and keep their children home from school. Others, however, may get up early, share breakfast together, and go to a special early service at their local mosque. Then they will go to work or school. They arrange to get together early in the evening to celebrate.

After the service there are parties and gatherings. The celebration continues for three days. People may gather at a mosque, local park or community centre. They visit or call their friends or family. They may also give gifts to friends and family members.

☾ Children sometimes receive small gifts of money, or even candies and toys.

During the three days of celebrations, Muslims share wonderful feasts. They often serve foods of their traditional heritage. Because Canadian Muslims

☪ **Eid ul-Fitr means delicious food!**

have their roots in many different regions such as Pakistan, South Asia and Saudi Arabia, this can mean enjoying Eid meals of many different varieties.

Delicious!

# Chapter 2

# Diwali

## A Festival of Lights

As the nights grow longer and colder, we know that soon Diwali (Dee-**wah**-lee) will be here! Diwali is also known as Divali (Dee-**vah**-lee) or Deepavali (Deep-**ah**-vah-**lee**). It is celebrated by Hindus, Sikhs and Jains around the world, including Canada. Diwali, Divali and Deepavali all mean "garland of lights." No wonder at Diwali time you see lights everywhere!

Hindus also follow a lunar calendar. Diwali falls on the date of the new moon between the months of Asvina and Kartika. In Canada, this date normally arrives in October or November. Diwali usually lasts for five days.

During Diwali, Hindus give thanks to Prince Rama. An ancient Indian poem, the *Ramayana*, tells how Prince Rama was forced to leave his home. He returned after 14 years of brave deeds and became the new king. Hindus light little oil lamps, called *diyas* (dee-yah), to celebrate his return.

A statue of Prince Rama

During Diwali, Sikhs remember one of their important leaders, Guru Hargobind Ji, and his release from captivity. To them, Diwali is a celebration of freedom. Jains remember Lord Mahavira. He was the founder of Jainism.

Hindus also honour Lakshmi during Diwali. Lakshmi is the goddess of wealth, luck and happiness. Families clean their houses and open their windows on the first night of Diwali, hoping that she will give them a special blessing. They also display beautiful flowers.

Sometimes families decorate their floors with designs made of coloured rice powder or crushed limestone. This art is called *rangoli*. The paintings are made in all corners of a home to honour and welcome Lakshmi.

Colourful *rangoli* patterns are placed in the corners of a home.

Many cultures believe that light represents goodness and happiness.

Most importantly, Hindus light up their homes during Diwali with *diya*s. This says to Lakshmi, "Please come in and visit our home!"

Families light *diyas* in their homes to honour Lakshmi.

To Hindus, Diwali is also the time when the old year ends and the new year begins. The third day of Diwali is the last day of the old year. On this night, lights are placed in the windows of Canadian homes, shops and temples. Lanterns may decorate porches and balconies.

Sikhs also light *diyas* at Diwali.
They pray for freedom from greed,
jealousy and anger.

The fourth morning of Diwali is the
new year. Many Hindu families
gather at their family altar. They
light candles and incense, and say a
prayer to Lakshmi. Then they go to
the temple for a special service. The
temple has been cleaned in honour
of Lakshmi. People bring gifts of
fruit to her. They bow and sing
songs to her. They pray that they
and their community will prosper.

Throughout the day, Hindu
worshippers get together with their
families or friends for a meal. They
may exchange gifts, such as candy
and clothes.

In some Canadian cities, like Toronto and Vancouver, there are public celebrations at city halls and community centres. People enjoy watching parades and music demonstrations. They might shop at bazaar booths or participate in workshops.

The celebrating continues into the evening. People wear fancy clothes. They dance and eat.

Diwali celebrations include dancing and music.

Many Hindu families have a small altar in their home where they honour Lakshmi all year. They place small candles and incense in front of her picture.

Outdoors, people set off fireworks. Children wave sparklers. Everyone celebrates the light. Traditionally, the loud noises are to scare away the bad spirits and allow only good luck to arrive in the new year.

On the fifth and last day of Diwali, brothers honour their sisters. They visit their sisters, share a meal with them and exchange gifts. Sisters express wishes for the long and happy lives of their brothers.

After Diwali ends, everyday life seems to return to normal, but Hindus hope that there is a little more light and understanding in the world.

Diwali fireworks at an outdoor celebration

# Chapter 3

# Chanukah

## Celebrating a Miracle

Jews around the world begin celebrating Chanukah (hah-neh-kah) on the 25th day of Kislev, according to the Hebrew calendar. It usually falls somewhere in December, late November or early January. Chanukah lasts for eight days. It is often called the Festival of Lights.

At Chanukah Jews remember an event that took place over 2000 years ago in what is now Israel. At the time, the Syrian-Greeks were rulers of the land. They had outlawed the Jewish faith. They took over the Jewish temple in the city of Jerusalem. They put up altars and idols in it and renamed it after their god, Zeus.

Led by Judah Maccabee, a group of Jews fought the Syrian-Greeks and took back their temple. They took down the altars and idols right away. They cleaned the temple and built a new altar.

Chanukah is a Hebrew word which means "dedication."

The Jews wanted to dedicate the temple to God once again. They needed to relight the temple's holy lamp, or menorah. The menorah was supposed to burn oil all night, every night, but there was only enough oil left for the lamp to burn for one day. Even so, they added the oil and lit the lamp.

The flame lasted for eight days and nights, which was enough time to make more oil. The Jews believed this was a miracle. They celebrate this miracle every year during the eight days of Chanukah.

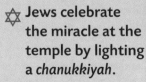 Jews celebrate the miracle at the temple by lighting a *chanukkiyah*.

Each night, beginning on the first night of the holiday, Jews light one candle for each of the days that the menorah burned in the temple. The special candleholder, or *chanukkiyah* (hah-neh-**keye**-yah), holds eight candles, plus one more, the *shammash*, which means "worker" or "servant."

On the first night, the *shammash* is lit and used to light the first candle. The *shammash* is then put in its place in the *chanukkiyah*, which is usually in the middle. The candles burn all night until they burn down to nothing.

During Chanukah, many Jews only eat foods that are allowed under Jewish law. For example, they are not permitted to eat milk and meat together.

On the second night, three new candles are used. The new *shammash* is lit and is used to light the second candle and then the first candle. This continues for eight days.

While the candles are being lit, the family members recite blessings or sing songs. Then they place the *chanukkiyah* in the windows of their homes.

✡ A *chanukkiyah* and torah, the Jewish holy book, in a window remind people passing of the holiday's miracle.

After the candles are lit, it is time to eat. Some people attend community parties or family dinners. Popular Chanukah foods such as jelly doughnuts or potato latkes are cooked in oil. The oil is a symbol of the oil that burned in the temple so long ago.

✡ Doughnuts are just one of the delicious foods eaten during Chanukah.

✡ Sometimes children are given *gelt* during Chanukah.

Some Jewish families celebrate on every night of Chanukah, and some celebrate on the first and last night. They might give the children little gifts, such as coins or chocolate coins called **gelt**.

# Dreidel Song

I have a little dreidel
I made it out of clay
And when it's dry and ready
Then dreidel I shall play!

Chorus:
Oh — dreidel, dreidel, dreidel
I made it out of clay
And when it's dry and ready
Then dreidel I shall play!

It has a lovely body
With legs so short and thin
And when my dreidel's tired
It drops and then I win!

Chorus

My dreidel's always playful
It loves to dance and spin
A happy game of dreidel
Come play now, let's begin!

Chorus

Children play games with dreidels (**dray**-dels), which are spinning tops with four sides. The Hebrew letters on the sides of a dreidel stand for "a great miracle happened there," meaning the miracle that took place in the temple in Israel.

After eight days, Chanukah ends. But for some time afterwards, many families might find themselves still humming the cheerful tune of the Dreidel Song.

✡ Children enjoy a game with dreidels.

# Chapter 4

# Christmas

## Celebrating the Birth of Christ

Many Christians around the world, including in Canada, celebrate Christmas on December 25. They recognize this day as the birthday of Jesus Christ, who they believe is the son of God.

The Bible, which is a holy book to Christians, tells the story of Christmas.

Over 2000 years ago in the town of Nazareth (in what is now Israel), the angel Gabriel appeared to a woman named Mary. He told Mary that she would give birth to the son of God.

Mary and her husband Joseph travelled to the town of Bethlehem. There was no room at any inn, so they stayed in a stable. There, Mary gave birth to Jesus. She placed him to sleep in a **manger**.

That night, a bright star appeared in the sky. Some shepherds, who had been told by an angel of Jesus' birth, followed the star. Three wise men also followed the star.

The shepherds and the wise men knew the baby was special, and they worshipped him.

🔔 Many people and churches mark the birth of Jesus with nativity scenes.

The kings brought Jesus gifts of gold, **frankincense and myrrh** (mer).

Christians believe God sent Jesus to Earth to teach people how to live good lives and to serve God. He brought them a message of the importance of loving one another. Christians believe that, because of Jesus, they too can be with God when they die.

To Christians, Christmas is a happy time of celebrating the birthday of Jesus and his message of love. Many people send good wishes to one another with Christmas cards. They may visit friends. They may gather to sing special songs, called carols, about the birth of Jesus.

Many Christians go to church at Christmas .

Many people put an evergreen tree in their homes at Christmastime. They decorate their Christmas tree with lights and ornaments. Some might put a star or angel on the top of the tree. This reminds them of the star that appeared in the sky to lead people to Jesus, or of the angel that appeared to the shepherds. They wrap gifts and put them under the tree. Later, they give them to one another, just as the wise men brought generous gifts to baby Jesus.

Many people who are not Christians also celebrate Christmas. They may put up Christmas trees, exchange gifts, and look forward to a visit from Santa Claus. They share in the happiness of the holiday.

Some Christians also give money or gifts to those in need. They believe it is important to make a special effort to share good things with others at Christmastime.

Some children believe that Santa Claus visits at Christmas. They believe Santa Claus lives at the North Pole and makes toys for children. The night before Christmas, while children sleep, Santa flies on his sled pulled by reindeer and visits every home. He brings gifts for children.

Some children leave out a snack of cookies or fruit for Santa Claus. He gets hungry on his busiest night of the year!

> **The tradition of Christmas trees began in Germany hundreds of years ago.**

On Christmas morning, families gather near their Christmas tree to exchange good wishes and to open presents. They may go to church. They greet friends and family with "Merry Christmas!"

Many Canadians spend the day relaxing with their families. In the evening, they get together with friends or relatives for a delicious Christmas dinner, such as turkey with cranberries and a special Christmas dessert.

Luckily, in Canada, the day after Christmas is also a holiday. Everyone has another day to relax and enjoy being together!

# Chapter 5

# Kwanzaa

## A Time for Reflection

For thousands of years, people in Africa worked hard to harvest their crops. When they were finished, they got together with their families and friends. They gave thanks for the food that they had gathered. They shared their fruits and vegetables. They rejoiced!

Today, a special celebration reminds us of these ancient harvests. It is celebrated from December 26 to January 1. The festival is called Kwanzaa.

Kwanzaa is observed in Canada, the United States, the Caribbean and the United Kingdom. "Kwanza" is a word in the African language of Swahili. It means "first." The extra 'a' was added to represent the seven-day celebration of the "first fruits." Just as people gather to celebrate the harvest, Kwanzaa is a time for family, friends and community to gather, share and reflect.

The Kwanzaa holiday started about 40 years ago. An African-American man named Dr. Maulana Karenga was very proud of his African ancestors. He admired their traditions and values. He wanted Africans in North America to remember and follow the ways of their ancestors. He thought this would help make the world a better place.

To get ready for Kwanzaa, people set up a display with symbols and may decorate their homes in red, black and green.

Families celebrate the ancient harvests.

| Symbol | What it symbolizes |
| --- | --- |
| *Mkeka* (em-**keh**-kah) straw mat | traditions |
| *Mazao* (mah-**zah**-oh) fruits and vegetables | first fruits/harvest; working together |
| *Muhindi* (moo-**heen**-dee) ears of corn | children, who are the hope for the future |
| *Kinara* (kee-**nah**-rah) candleholder | the first African men and women |
| *Mishumma Saba* (mee-shoo-**mah sah**-bah) the seven candles | the seven principles/ days of Kwanzaa |
| *Kikombe cha Umoja* (kee-**kohm**-bay chah oo-**mo**-jah) unity cup | togetherness (unity) |
| *Zawadi* (zah-**wah**-dee) gifts | the labour and love of parents; promises kept by the children |

During Kwanzaa, people share their family history with one another and celebrate their pride in their black heritage. They prepare and eat wonderful meals. Often the food is from different parts of Africa. It might even be food from a different country each night!

Kwanzaa is also a time to think about how to be a better person. There are seven days of Kwanzaa, and there is one important belief for each day. On each day, people think about that day's belief. They try to make it their goal for that day. They also hope they will work at making it part of their everyday lives in the future.

# The Seven Principles

**Day One:** *Umoja* (oo-**mo**-jah) Unity ⊠
Keep unity in the family and community. Stick together with your friends and neighbours. Work and play together. Try to live in peace.

**Day Two:** *Kujichagulia* (koo-jee-chah-**goo**-lee-ah) Self-Determination ⊞
Make good decisions and set goals for yourself. Believe in yourself. Be responsible for the things you do.

**Day Three:** *Ujima* (oo-**jee**-mah) Collective Work and Responsibility ✖
Work together with others and help others. Make a better community.

**Day Four:** *Ujamaa* (oo-jah-**mah**-ah) Using Money Cooperatively ⧗
Use money well so that everyone is better off. Think about others when you spend money. Buy things together.

**Day Five:** *Nia* (**nee**-ah) Purpose ⏐

Plan ahead. Think about your actions and the consequences. Do things for a reason. Look back at your history for inspiration. Help others reach their goals.

**Day Six:** *Kuumba* (koo-**oom**-bah) Creativity ⚘

Show how you feel and what you believe by drawing, dancing and painting. Do what you can to make your community more beautiful. Think without any boundaries. Also, make your home beautiful. Celebrate your talents!

**Day Seven:** *Imani* (ee-**mah**-nee) Faith ☥

Believe in your family and yourself, your teachers and leaders. Believe in your people.

Every evening, families gather together for a special ceremony around the Kwanzaa display. Fruits, vegetables and ears of corn, one for each child in the family, are placed on a straw mat. There is also a candleholder with places for seven candles, one for each day of Kwanzaa.

Families set out the Kwanzaa symbols.

Each night, a child in the family lights a candle. One candle is lit the first night, two candles are lit the second night, and so on. The family talks about the belief of the day. They all take a sip from the unity cup. After they eat together, they may give one another a *zawadi*, or gift, representing their history or culture. It is often handmade.

Usually, on the last day of Kwanzaa, a *karamu* (kah-**rah**-moo), or feast, is held. On this night, there is a very big party. People share a feast at one another's homes or go out to restaurants in large groups. People dance or tell stories or give speeches. They celebrate their ancestors, and they dream about the future. They promise to look after one another and to live good lives. And they have lots of fun!

# Chapter 6

# Chinese New Year

## Kung Hay Fat Choy!

"Kung hay fat choy! Kung hay fat choy!"

Everyone along the parade route is calling out these words. This is Cantonese for "May you become prosperous!"

The Chinese New Year is the most important Chinese holiday. It is celebrated on the first day of the Chinese year. The Chinese calendar is based on the moon and sun. There are 12 months in each year.

Chinese New Year falls some time between January and February. Each year is named for one of 12 animals: rat, ox, tiger, rabbit, dragon, serpent, horse, ram, monkey, rooster, dog and boar.

A few days before the new year, families clean and dust their homes, sweeping out the old and welcoming in the new.

**To the Chinese, red is the colour of good luck and happiness.**

Families put out pyramids of fruit, like oranges and red apples.

Decorations with special good luck words are hung in homes.

They hang red decorations with writing that says: "Good luck! Long life!"

Families also say goodbye to their kitchen god at this time. Traditionally, a kitchen god lives in everyone's house. At the end of the year, this spirit leaves to report to the heavens about the behaviour of the people in the house. Families put out sweet foods, such as oranges and sugar cane. They hope the kitchen god will say only sweet things about them!

On New Year's Eve, families write lucky words or sayings with a gold pen on red paper and put them throughout the house. The whole family gets together for a special dinner. They are careful to leave some food uneaten. This "lucky" food is saved and eaten on New Year's Day.

An ancient Chinese legend tells about a beast, Nian, that would silently enter people's homes on New Year's Eve — and eat them. It was discovered that Nian was scared of loud noises and the colour red. People began setting off fireworks and explosions, and decorating their homes in red on this one night of the year. When Nian ran away, the people would rejoice. It is said that this is how the first New Year celebrations began.

Everyone stays awake until midnight, even the youngest children. Then they go to the marketplace. At twelve o'clock, fireworks are set off. The kitchen god is welcomed back. Young people bow to the adults to show respect. They are given small red envelopes called *lai see* (leye see). They contain good luck money.

Red envelopes containing money, as well as sweets, are laid out during Chinese New Year.

On New Year's Day, the first day of the new year, good luck arrives! All cleaning stops. No one wants to sweep away the good luck! People feel like they are making a fresh start. They celebrate a new beginning. Celebrating old traditions links them to their ancestors and the past.

Everyone tries to say and do good things during the new year celebrations. Tradition says that what they do on this day will decide what happens to them the rest of the year.

People put on new clothes. They visit their grandparents and then their friends. They share gifts and food. They think about their ancestors. "Kung hay fat choy!" they call to one another.

The new year's holiday normally lasts for fifteen days. On the seventh day, everyone celebrates their birthday. The fifteenth day is Chinese Valentine's Day. Everyone gets together to celebrate. There are lanterns everywhere! During this time, people enjoy dragon parades, more fireworks, and finally a beautiful lantern festival. It's time to celebrate!

Children dress up to perform during the new year celebrations.

# Glossary

**chanukkiyah:** a nine-branched candle holder used during Chanukah

**diya:** a small, clay oil lamp

**Eid Mubarak:** a greeting said during Eid ul-Fitr that means "Blessed Eid"

**fajr:** a Muslim morning prayer

**fast:** to go without food or drink for a period of time

**frankincense and myrrh:** sweet-smelling gum resin used for burning as incense

**karamu:** a feast held during Kwanzaa

**gelt:** money

**iftar:** an evening when Muslims can break their fast during Ramadan, usually done with family

**lunar calendar:** a calendar that is based on the cycle of the moon

**manger:** a small box in a barn which animals eat from

**mosque:** a place of worship for Muslims

**rangoli:** a floor painting of coloured powder common among some East Indians, made up of geometric shapes

**shammash:** the candle in the middle of the *chanukkiyah* used to light the other candles at Chanukah

**lai see:** small red envelopes containing money given during Chinese New Year

**Zakat-ul-Fitr:** a donation or gift to charity that is given during Ramadan

**zawadi:** a gift, often handmade, given during Kwanzaa